High Society Sandwiches

100 Classic Afternoon Tea Sandwich Recipes (Annotated)

Sarah Rorer

Contents

As a thank you for purchasing this book, we wanted to send you a bonus free gift.

You can get instant access to the

Vintage Tea Party Recipe Book

by going to

www.howtohightea.com/bonus

Author's Note

In Regency times in London, Afternoon Tea was a major part of the Season when debutants were presented at court. The romance of these events also captivated many in America where Afternoon tea events became popular social events. Guests would come for a few hours to enjoy each other's company, gossip and of course to eat afternoon delicacies. This book is filled with over one hundred classic Afternoon tea sandwich recipes from these times. Every recipe has been updated and modernized so you can recreate the same classic recipes of the Regency Afternoon Teas with ease and grace that will no doubt impress your guests.

Be inspired by these classic recipes to create an Afternoon Tea Event. Afternoon tea events are fantastic for small family parties, weddings, bridal showers, baby showers and many more happy occasions. The classic sandwich recipes in this book are perfect for any event, as we have carefully checked, updated and added further inspiration to Sarah's original recipes from 1894. Now we can all continue to enjoy her exquisite taste in sandwich fillings for exceptional Afternoon Tea Events.

The Classic Afternoon Tea Recipes in this book are adapted for our modern kitchens, modern measurements and ovens. In many cases, we have changed methods to ones that are more efficient and in keeping with modern times. At all times we have aimed to make these fabulous traditional recipes into quick, easy to make sandwiches, without losing the special character that made these recipes so popular. Our changes will ensure you will find these fabulous recipes are easy, simple and quick to make. Surprise your guests with a wide range of delicious sandwiches that will delight and inspire many more afternoon tea events.

1

While sandwiches may be made from any sliced bread, the most popular at events are those made with whole wheat bread or white bread.

2

Always butter the bread before adding a filling. The butter needs to be slightly softened first and may be seasoned with a dash of paprika, a little white pepper, and a few drops of Worcestershire sauce.

3

For ordinary sandwiches use untoasted bread. For canapés, lightly toasted bread is preferred.

4

Sandwiches are principally used for buffet lunches or evening social events, where only a light meal is required. Although, sandwiches can be made in a great variety of flavors to suit any event or time of the day.

5

Afternoon Tea Sandwiches can be cut into squares, triangles, long fingers, rounds or crescent shapes. One slice of bread will usually make one round sandwich and one crescent.

6

If meat is used for sandwiches, it should be chopped very fine and slightly moistened with cream, melted butter, olive oil or mayonnaise dressing that has been well seasoned. In many of the recipes we suggest using a blender to chop the meat finely and combine with the cream or butter.

* Sarah notes here that Turkey, chicken, game, tongue, beef and mutton, with their proper seasonings, moistened with either mayonnaise or French dressing, also make exceedingly nice sandwiches.

7

Cooked fish can be rubbed or pounded in a mortar with tartare sauce to make it moist enough to easily spread on the bread. We suggest using a blender to chop the fish and combine with the sauce.

8

As an alternative to sliced bread in any of the recipes, small French rolls may be used. Scoop out the bread in the center and fill the space with the sandwich mix.

9

When served with coffee, sandwiches make an attractive meal that is easily served and can be enjoyed by all. Enjoy!

When hosting an event, one needs to make sandwiches several hours before they are needed. The risk of doing this is that sandwiches can dry out very quickly, making for stale and unattractive sandwiches that are not enjoyable to eat. The best way to avoid this is to make sandwiches as close to the time of the event as possible.

It is possible to make sandwiches a few hours before an event, but these must be carefully wrapped to keep them fresh or they will become unpalatable. We suggest placing the sandwiches on large plates or trays and covering with plastic cling foil and keeping them in the fridge or a cool room.

Sarah had a trick she liked to use back in the days before household refrigerators. Her preferred way for keeping sandwiches moist was this:

Wet two ordinary tea towels and wring them out fully. Lay these damp tea towels out on the bench. As Sarah made her sandwiches, she would put them on top of the damp towel; when she had the desired quantity made, she would cover the top with moist lettuce leaves and fold over the towels. Then she would cover the entire thing with a dry cloth. She found that sandwiches prepared in this way would keep for several hours in perfectly good condition. On a very warm day she would additionally cover them with even more moist lettuce leaves.

Savory High Society Sandwiches

The Captain's Anchovy Sandwiches

Instructions

Cream a quarter of a pound of butter.

Gradually add two tablespoons of lemon juice, a teaspoon of paprika and two tablespoons of anchovy paste.

Mix well.

Spread the anchovy mixture on thin slices of bread.

Put two slices of bread together and trim off the crusts.

Cut sandwiches into triangles to serve.

The Captain's Anchovy and Egg Sandwiches

Instructions

Mash the yolks of four hard-boiled eggs with two tablespoons of melted butter or olive oil.

Add a half teaspoon of salt, a dash of paprika and a tablespoon of anchovy paste.

Spread this mixture between thin slices of buttered bread.

Press the slices together and trim off the crusts.

Cut into triangles.

*Sardines may be used in the place of anchovies.

The Duke of Wellington's Beef Sandwiches

Instructions

Finely chop half a pound of cold roasted beef and put it into a bowl.

Add a half teaspoon of salt, a tablespoon of tomato ketchup, a teaspoon of Worcestershire sauce and a teaspoon of melted butter to the meat.

Mix well to combine.

If you prefer a smoother mixture, combine all ingredients in a blender.

Spread the mixture over slices of bread.

Put two slices together, and cut into desired shapes to serve.

Basic Bread and Butter Sandwiches

Instructions

Cream the desired amount of butter.

Butter each slice of bread and roll it.

The rolls of buttered bread may be tied with a narrow baby ribbon or wrapped in waxed paper, fringing and twisting the ends.

Royal Academy Caviar Sandwiches No. 1

Instructions

Cream a quarter of a pound of butter.

Add two tablespoons of crushed onions, two teaspoons of lemon juice, and a dash of paprika.

Mix together.

Gradually and gently fold into the mixture four tablespoons of caviar.

Spread the caviar mixture on thin slices of brown bread or pumpernickel bread.

Put two slices together and press lightly.

Cut into long, narrow shapes to serve.

Royal Academy Caviar Sandwiches No. 2

Instructions

Cut slices of bread into crescent-shaped pieces and lightly toast. Butter one side.

Mash the yolks of two hard-boiled eggs and set them aside.

Finely chop the egg whites and set them aside in another dish.

Spread the slices of toast with a layer of caviar; then sprinkle over the chopped egg whites, then a little of the mashed yolks.

Garnish with sliced onion.

Serve the toasts open without a second slice of bread on top.

Ashley House Celery Sandwiches

Instructions

Lightly toast thin slices of bread. Butter one side.

Cut the white part of celery into thin slices and layer this on the toasts.

Cover the celery with a layer of mayonnaise dressing and with another piece of toast.

Cut into squares and serve.

Cheltenham Celery Salad Sandwiches

Instructions

Hard-boil four eggs.

Take the white portion from one head of celery; wash and chop it very fine.

Finely chop the hard-boiled eggs.

Mix the eggs and the celery together, adding a half teaspoon of salt and a dash of pepper.

Layer the mixed egg and celery on thin slices of bread.

Place a teaspoon of mayonnaise dressing in the center, and smooth it all over.

Put the two pieces of bread together and press them lightly.

Trim off the crusts, and cut the sandwiches into fingers about two inches wide to serve.

Chelsea Chicken Sandwiches (Rolled)

For the chicken mixture:

Finely chop cold chicken and put aside.

Rub together two tablespoons of butter and two tablespoons of flour in a saucepan.

Slowly add half a cup of hot milk, while gently heating and stirring constantly.

When fully combined and the butter is melted, add the chicken, a level teaspoon of salt, a half teaspoon of celery seed, a teaspoon of white pepper, a dash of red pepper, a teaspoon of onion juice and a grating of nutmeg.

Mix and allow to cool.

Making the Sandwiches:

Butter each slice of bread and spread with the chicken mixture.

Roll the sandwiches and wrap them immediately in waxed paper.

Chicken Sandwiches A la Rorer

Instructions

Finely chop cooked chicken.

Finely chop two bunches of cress with a sharp knife.

Wash and dry the crisp portion from a head of lettuce.

Put the yolks of two eggs into a double-boiler saucepan, add the juice from two lemons and stir over hot water until the mixture is thick; remove from heat and slowly add two tablespoons of olive oil.

Add this warm mixture to the chicken and season with a half teaspoon of salt and a dash of pepper.

Butter thin slices of bread and cover with a thick layer of the chicken mixture. Add a thin slice of brown bread, buttered on both sides; cover this with a thick layer of cress, dust it lightly with salt and pepper, then add another slice of white bread, buttered.

Press the slices firmly together, trim the crusts and cut into fingers to serve.

Convent Garden Chicken and Almond Sandwiches

Instructions

Chop cold cooked chicken.

Chop a quarter of a pound of blanched almonds.

Combine the almonds and the chicken.

Add four tablespoons of cream, a half teaspoon of salt and a dash of pepper.

Mix thoroughly.

Spread on thin slices of buttered bread and add another slice on top.

Press gently together and cut into crescents or rounds to serve.

Countess Kendall's Chicken and Lettuce Sandwiches

Instructions

Chop cold chicken.

Mix the chicken together with the hard-boiled yolks of four eggs, four tablespoons of thick cream, a half teaspoon of salt, a dash of pepper, and two teaspoons of celery seed.

Butter thin slices of white bread. Spread the mixture on the slices of bread. Place on top a slice of brown bread buttered on both sides.

Add a thick layer of shredded celery, with a tablespoon of mayonnaise in the middle. Add another slice of buttered white bread on top.

Press the slices gently together. Trim the crusts and cut them into fingers to serve.

Princess's Chicken Sandwiches

Instructions

Finely chop cold cooked chicken.

Add the juice of half a lemon, two tablespoons of melted butter or olive oil, twelve walnuts finely chopped, a half teaspoon of paprika and a half teaspoon of salt.

Mix well.

Spread the mixture between thin slices of buttered bread.

Trim the crusts and cut them into fingers to serve.

Windsor Chicken Sandwiches

These are especially popular to serve at afternoon teas. If well made, they are the most elaborate and dainty of all sandwiches.

Instructions

Finely chop cold cooked chicken. Add a half cupful of finely chopped celery, a half teaspoon of salt, a dash of pepper and four tablespoons of cream. Mix well and set aside.

Chop baked ham into small cubes. Add a tablespoon of tomato ketchup, a few drops of Worcestershire sauce and a dash of pepper. Mix well and set aside.

Shred one head of Romaine lettuce or a bunch of cress. (This of course must be crisp and dry.) Spread a layer of the chicken mixture on the buttered side of a slice of bread. Add on top another slice of buttered bread.

To this add a thick layer of ham mixture and sprinkle with the shredded cress or Romaine lettuce. Add a final thin slice of bread.

Press the bread slices firmly together and cut into fingers. Wrap in waxed paper or tie with baby ribbon.

Almack's Tea Biscuit Sandwiches

Instructions

Sift four cups of flour into a bowl. Add four level teaspoonfuls of baking powder and a teaspoon of salt.

Rub in two tablespoons of butter and add sufficient milk to make a dough.

This dough must not be soft, but must be sufficiently stiff to handle quickly. Add extra flour if necessary.

Knead the dough quickly and roll into a sheet a quarter of an inch thick.

Cut into good-sized round biscuits; they must be at least two and a half to three inches in diameter. Brush the biscuits with milk.

Bake the biscuits for 20 to 25 minutes at 200c or until golden and well risen. Transfer to a wire rack to cool.

When cool, cut the center from each biscuit, leaving a wall one inch thick.

Fill this space with the following deviled chicken mix.

Devilled Chicken Mix

Instructions

Finely chop cooked chicken.

Add eight tablespoons of melted butter, cream or olive oil, a dash of cayenne, a dash of white pepper, a teaspoon of celery seed and a teaspoon of paprika.

Mix well.

Fill the tea biscuits with this mixture.

Add a small garnish of parsley.

Serve immediately.

Upper Rooms Swiss Cheese Sandwiches

Instructions

Butter thin slices of pumpernickel or brown bread

Place a very thin layer of Swiss cheese between the slices.

Gently press the two slices together.

Cut into triangles.

Garnish with cress to serve.

Lady Daphne's Cheese Sandwiches

Instructions

Finely chop a quarter of a pound of soft American cheese and place in a saucepan.

Beat the yolk of one egg with two tablespoons of cream, a dash of salt, a dash of red pepper and half a teaspoon of Worcestershire sauce.

Add the egg mixture to the cheese.

Heat gently until the cheese is completely melted. Remove from heat and cool.

Butter thin slices of bread. Spread the cooled mixture on the slices of bread.

Cover with another slice of buttered bread and press together. Cut into rounds or crescents to serve.

The Polo Club's Cheese Sandwiches

Instructions

Blend together one tablespoon of butter, two tablespoons of soft club-house cheese, a tablespoon of grated Parmesan, a teaspoon of salt, and a teaspoon of anchovy paste.

Add a teaspoon of tarragon vinegar and a half teaspoon of pepper.

Lightly toast thin slices of white bread. Spread cheese mixture on one slice, cover it with another.

Cut the sandwiches into round or crescent shapes to serve.

Saville Row Cheese Sandwiches

Instructions

Blend half a pint of cottage cheese with two tablespoons of melted butter, a half teaspoon of salt and two tablespoons of thick cream.

Beat until smooth and light.

Spread the cheese mixture thickly on slices of brown bread.

Add a very thin slice of white bread on top of the cheese.

Add more of the cheese mixture and finish with a slice of the brown bread.

Press together. Cut into fingers to serve.

Count Elliot Cheese Sandwiches

Instructions

Grate half a pound of Swiss cheese.

Combine with the cooked yolks of two eggs.

Add four tablespoons of olive oil, a dash of cayenne and a half teaspoon of salt.

Blend together until you have a perfectly smooth paste.

Put this mixture between layers of buttered rye bread and serve.

Do not trim the crusts nor cut.

Countess of Cleves Cheese Sandwiches

Instructions

Blend together two Spanish sweet peppers (pimientos), one Neufchatel cheese, one pared and quartered apple and twelve blanched almonds.

Add a half teaspoon of salt and a half teaspoon of paprika.

Spread the mixture between thin slices of buttered white or brown bread.

Press gently together.

Cut the crusts and cut into fingers to serve.

Cheltenham Cheese Spice Sandwiches

Ingredients

1 pound of American cheese

1 cup of thick sour cream

1 teaspoon of Worcestershire sauce

1 tablespoon of tomato ketchup

1 teaspoon of salt

1 teaspoon of paprika

Instructions

Grate the American cheese.

Gradually add the sour cream to the grated cheese. Use a blender to make a smooth mix.

Add all the other ingredients to this mixture and blend well.

Spread on thin slices of buttered bread. Cover the mixture with chopped cress.

Add another slice of bread. Press the slices gently together.

Trim off the crusts.

Cut into triangles to serve.

Instructions

Grate a half-pound of American cheese.

Add one Neufchatel cheese.

Mix well.

Add one peeled, chopped tomato, one finely chopped sweet red pepper, a half teaspoon of salt and a little black pepper.

Mix well.

Spread this mixture between slices of white bread, or you may use one slice of white with one slice of whole-wheat bread.

These are usually served cut into rounds with an ordinary cake cutter. If you cut these economically you can make one good-sized round sandwich and a crescent from each, or if you use a very small cutter you should make four round sandwiches.

Lady Curry Sandwiches

Instructions

Blend one Neufchatel or Philadelphia cream cheese to a paste.

Add one pimiento, chopped fine; a dozen almonds, a dozen pecan nuts; a tablespoon of tomato ketchup, a level teaspoon of curry and two tablespoons of desiccated grated coconut.

Blend thoroughly, adding sufficient olive oil to make a smooth paste.

Spread between thin, unbuttered slices of white bread.

Trim the crusts and cut into long fingers.

These are nice to serve with plain lettuce salad at dinner.

Derby Deviled Cheese Sandwiches

Instructions

Grate one pound of American cheese.

Blend together with two tablespoons of tomato ketchup, one teaspoon of Worcestershire sauce, a half teaspoon of paprika, a dash of cayenne, two tablespoons of olive oil or melted butter, four tablespoons of sherry and a half teaspoon of salt.

Mix until perfectly smooth.

Spread between thin slices of buttered bread.

Trim the crusts and cut into triangles to serve.

Marquis Roquefort Cheese Sandwiches

Instructions

Blend a quarter of a pound of Roquefort cheese.

Gradually add sufficient melted butter to make a paste.

Spread this between slices of buttered bread.

Press the slices together.

Trim the crusts, and cut into fingers to serve.

House of Parliament Camembert Sandwiches

Instructions

Spread softened Camembert cheese between slices of buttered whole wheat bread.

Trim the crusts.

Cut into shapes to serve.

Prince Regent Corned Beef Sandwiches

Instructions

Chop sufficient cold cooked corned beef to make two cups.

Add a teaspoon of horseradish, four tablespoons of melted butter or olive oil and four or five tablespoons of finely shredded watercress.

Put this between slices of buttered whole wheat or brown bread.

Trim the crusts and cut into triangles to serve.

These may be served after lunch with coffee, or are exceedingly nice for picnics or for afternoons where coffee is served.

Kensington Cottage Cheese Sandwiches

These are nice for country picnics.

Instructions

The cottage cheese should be drained and quite dry, moisten it by adding either thick cream or melted butter; do not make it too soft.

Add a dash of black pepper and a palatable seasoning of salt.

Spread between slices of buttered whole wheat or white bread.

Press the two slices together.

Trim the crusts and cut into shapes to serve.

Marchioness Cucumber Lettuce Sandwiches

Instructions

Slice cucumber into very thin slices.

Layer these slices on thin slices of buttered bread.

Finely shred lettuce and put this over the cucumber, add a layer of chopped cooked chicken.

Sprinkle over more shredded lettuce and a little mayonnaise on top of this.

Add another slice of buttered bread.

Press the two slices together.

Trim the crusts.

Cut into shapes and serve on a napkin in a pretty wicker basket.

Regency Cucumber Sandwiches

These are very nice to serve with a fish course in place of bread or rolls and a salad.

Instructions

Slice the cucumbers very thin and soak them in ice water for one or two hours. They must be crisp and brittle and made just at serving time.

Beat together three tablespoons of olive oil, one tablespoon of vinegar, a dash of salt and a dash of pepper; place in the fridge until it thickens.

Butter thin slices of bread, cover them with a layer of cucumbers that have been drained and dried on a napkin, sprinkle over the dressing.

Add another layer of buttered bread. Press the slices of bread together.

Trim the crusts and cut into triangles to serve.

Dandy Curried Oyster Sandwiches

Instructions

Cover a buttered slice of bread with a thin layer of mashed hard-boiled egg. In the center of this sandwich put the soft parts of six pickled oysters.

Put a tablespoon of butter and a tablespoon of flour into a little saucepan; mix without melting. Add half a cup of thick cream, a teaspoon of onion juice and a teaspoon of curry and half a teaspoon of turmeric.

Bring to the boil. Remove from heat and beat together. Set aside to cool.

When you are ready to serve the sandwiches, cover each buttered slice with a thin layer of this sauce. Place another slice of bread on top.Press together, and serve.

The sauce must not go over the sandwiches until you are ready to serve. Use the sauce sparingly so it does not soak through the bread.

*A note on pickled oysters: Pickled oysters were very popular in the United States around the turn-of the-century (late 1800s and early 1900s).

Instructions

Shuck four dozen oysters and put them, along with their juice into a sauté pan.

Simmer over medium heat until they begin to curl around the edges.

Using a slotted spoon, remove the cooked oysters and plunge into a bowl of ice cubes and cold water to stop the cooking process; drain the oysters and set aside.

Combine 8 whole peppercorns, 1 teaspoon of salt, a dash of ground mace, 3 tablespoons of white wine, ¼ cup of vinegar or lemon juice, 2 tablespoons of sherry, and 6 drops of Tabasco sauce to the hot oyster liquor.

Simmer over low for 10 minutes. Remove from the heat and let cool.

Put the cooked oysters into a quart container with a lid and pour the cooled pickling sauce over them. Cover tightly and refrigerate at least 24 hours before serving to allow the flavors to blend.

These pickled oysters will keep in the refrigerator for up to 5 days.

Ramsgate Curried Egg Sandwiches

Instructions

Hard boil four eggs. Remove the yolks from the whites.

Chop the whites very, very fine and set aside.

Mash the yolks and gradually mix with four tablespoons of melted butter or olive oil, a half teaspoon of salt, a teaspoon of onion juice and a half teaspoon of curry.

Mix until smooth. Spread a thin layer of the yolk mixture over buttered slices of bread.

Add a layer of the chopped whites and another slice of buttered bread.

Press together. Trim the crusts and cut into shapes to serve.

Cotillion Curried Sardine Sandwiches

Instructions

Remove the heads, tails and bones from one large tin of sardines.

Blend them to a paste, adding a tablespoon of melted butter, a half teaspoon of curry powder and a teaspoon of salt.

Spread this mixture between slices of buttered bread.

Press the two slices of bread together.

Trim the crusts and cut into shapes to serve.

King's Theatre Curried Chicken Sandwiches

Instructions

Finely chop cold cooked chicken.

In saucepan rub together one tablespoon of butter and one tablespoon of flour; add a half cup of cold milk.

Heat and stir until it becomes a smooth, thick paste. Remove from heat.

In a blender, combine the warm mixture with the chicken.

Add a level teaspoon curry powder, a half-teaspoon of salt, half a chopped onion and a teaspoon of lemon juice.

Blend thoroughly and allow to cool.

When cold, spread between layers of buttered bread. Trim the crusts and cut into shapes to serve.

Almost any bits of left-over meat may be substituted for the chicken and made into sandwiches of this kind.

Instructions

Remove the meat from six hard-boiled crabs.

Mix with four tablespoons of mayonnaise.

Spread mixture between thin slices of bread and butter.

Press the two slices together.

Trim off the crusts.

Cut into triangles and serve.

Crab and lobster sandwiches should not be allowed to stand for more than an hour, and then must be wrapped carefully in a clean, damp cloth or kept refrigerated.

Le Dame Cream of Chicken Sandwiches

Instructions

Blend half cup of cold cooked chicken until it is a paste.

Put a teaspoon of granulated gelatin with two tablespoons of cold water in a pan, and heat until dissolved.

Whip a half pint of cream to a stiff froth.

Pour the gelatin into the chicken paste. Add a teaspoon of grated horseradish and a half teaspoon of salt. Stir until it begins to thicken, cool. Slowly combine with the whipped cream. Chill in the fridge for an hour.

When ready to make the sandwiches, cover each buttered slice of bread with this cream mixture. Trim off the crusts and cut sandwiches into fancy shapes. Garnish the top with olives cut into rings.

In the center of each sandwich add a little mound of capers, using the olives at the four corners; each sandwich may be garnished in a different way. Little pieces of celery, with the white top attached, make also a pretty garnish. These sandwiches are served as open sandwiches without a second slice of bread on top.

Duchess of York Sandwiches

Instructions

Chop a quarter of a pound of cold, corned beef very fine.

Add two tablespoons of olive oil, a dash of red pepper, a teaspoon of Worcestershire sauce, and a teaspoon of paprika.

Mix well.

Add the mashed hard-boiled yolks of three eggs.

Put this between thin slices of bread and butter.

Garnish with watercress to serve.

Duke of Clarence Beef Sandwiches

Instructions

Chop remains of cold cooked beef very fine.

For every two cups of beef, add one tablespoon of tomato ketchup, a dash of cayenne, two tablespoons of melted butter, a teaspoon of Worcestershire sauce, a half teaspoonful of paprika and a tablespoon of crushed onion.

Rub to a paste or use a blender to make a smooth mixture.

Spread this mixture on thin slices of buttered bread.

Trim off the crusts and cut into triangles to serve.

Instructions

Blend boiled lentils until smooth.

To each half-cup of this mixture add a half-cup of chopped pecans, a level teaspoon of curry and a half-teaspoon of salt.

Spread mixture on thin slices of buttered brown bread.

Cover with chopped parsley.

Cover with another slice of brown bread.

Press slices together.

Trim the crusts and cut into fingers to serve.

Imperial Egg Sandwiches

Instructions

Mash the yolks of six hard-boiled eggs.

Gradually add two tablespoons of olive oil or thick cream.

Add a dash of paprika and one-half teaspoon of salt.

Spread this mixture between thin slices of bread and butter.

Cut into fingers.

Garnish with watercress to serve.

Tea Room Egg Sandwiches

Instructions

Thinly slice hard-boiled eggs.

Layer these slices between slices of brown bread and butter.

Dust the egg slightly with salt and pepper.

Trim the edges of the sandwiches with either cress or lettuce.

Cut into triangles or squares to serve.

Bonny Charley Sandwiches

Instructions

These are nice for porch suppers, and may be served with either tea, coffee or hot chocolate.

Butter thin slices of bread and remove the crusts.

Lay a crisp lettuce leaf on one half the buttered slices, and spread with sandwich dressing (recipe below).

Add another slice of buttered bread.

Press the two slices together.

Cut into triangles to serve.

*Watercress, Romaine, or bleached chicory may be used in place of lettuce.

Regency Sandwich Dressing

Instructions

Put four tablespoons of vinegar and three of water into a saucepan.

Heat and add half a teaspoon of salt and half a teaspoon of pepper.

Beat the yolks of four eggs until creamy, and slowly add to the hot mixture.

Stir until it is the consistency of mayonnaise dressing.

Take from the heat and add two level tablespoons of butter.

Stir until the butter is melted.

Duchess of Manchester Egg Sandwiches

Instructions

Boil six eggs.

Remove from heat and put into cold water.

Remove the shells and cut eggs into slices lengthwise.

Butter thins slices of bread and cover with the slices of hard-boiled eggs.

Dust lightly with salt and pepper.

Spread Regency sandwich dressing over the eggs.

Lay a small piece of lettuce or cress over the dressing.

Add another slice of buttered bread.

Press the two slices together and cut into triangles to serve.

Marchioness of Abercorn Sandwiches

Instructions

Add one tin of crushed, drained pineapple to a cup of peanut butter.

Mix thoroughly.

Add a tablespoon of lemon juice, a dash of cayenne, a half teaspoon of paprika.

Put this between thin slices of buttered brown bread.

Press together and cut into halves to serve.

Captain Cook Sandwiches

Instructions

Blend a quarter of a pound of cold, boiled fish to a paste.

Add half a teaspoon of Worcestershire sauce, a tablespoon of olive oil, a half teaspoon of salt, and a half teaspoon of black pepper.

Trim off the crusts from the bread slices, and butter.

On each slice layer dainty lettuce leaves.

Fill the center with the fish mixture.

Cover with another layer of buttered bread from which you have trimmed the crusts, and press the two together.

Cut into fingers to serve.

Mayfair Sandwiches

Instructions

Flake cold boiled white fish.

Dust it with salt and pepper and sprinkle it with lemon juice.

Spread a layer of thin crisp cucumber on thin slices of brown bread.

Spread the flaked fish on top of the cucumber.

Put a tablespoon of mayonnaise in the center of the slice.

Add another layer of chopped watercress.

Finally add another slice of buttered brown bread.

Press together and cut into halves to serve.

Savile Row Sandwiches

Instructions

Flake cold cooked fish.

Dust it with salt, pepper and lemon juice.

Rub the bottom of a bowl with a clove of garlic.

Add half a cup of mayonnaise, four finely chopped gherkins, twelve chopped olives and two tablespoons of capers.

Mix and stir in two tablespoons of finely chopped parsley.

Spread a thin layer of this dressing over a plain slice of bread.

Spread this with the fish.

Add a crisp lettuce leaf, then cover with another slice of bread that has been spread with the dressing.

Press, trim the crusts and cut into fingers to serve.

Instructions

Flake one can of salmon.

Add to it a half teaspoon of salt, a dash of cayenne and one ordinary cucumber, grated and drained.

Butter thin slices of bread.

Spread a layer of the flaked fish on the slices.

Add a thin layer of mayonnaise or Regency sandwich dressing.

Cover with another slice of bread.

Press together and trim the crusts.

Cut directly across the slice, making two long sandwiches about an inch and a half to two inches wide.

Serve with a garnish of parsley.

Lady Grey Sandwiches

Instructions

Blend the white meat of one chicken to a paste.

Add one-half teaspoon of salt and a dash of red pepper.

In a pan combine one tablespoon of gelatin and a tablespoon of cold water.

Soak it for about five minutes.

Add ten tablespoons of thickened cream. Heat slowly until the gelatin is dissolved.

Blend together with the chicken mix. Chill for an hour.

Spread the cold mixture on thin slices of buttered bread.

Cover this with another slice of bread and cut into shapes.

Garnish with cress or parsley to serve.

Count Limburg Sandwiches

Instructions

Butter thin slices of rye bread.

Spread each slice with a thin layer of limburger cheese.

Cut bologna sausage into the thinnest possible slices.

Cover the limburger cheese with the sliced bologna.

Add a thin slice of pumpernickel or rye bread

Cover with another slice of bread that has been coated with a layer of cheese.

Press the slices together; do not remove the crusts.

Serve on a napkin in a wicker basket.

Note: Limburger Cheese is a semi-soft spreadable cheese. You can substitute for another spreadable cheese.

Blue Bonnet Sandwiches

Instructions

Finely chop cooked ham.

For each cup of ham stir in two tablespoons of melted butter, a small amount of red pepper and one-half teaspoon of crushed onion.

Butter thin slices of bread and remove the crusts.

Spread with the ham paste.

Cut into fingers.

Serve with watercress garnishing.

Viscount Lettuce Sandwiches

Instructions

Take the white part of a lettuce, wash and wipe it perfectly dry.

Mash the yolks of three hard-boiled eggs and make into a paste with four tablespoons of thickened cream.

Add one-half tablespoon of lemon juice.

Stir in four tablespoons of whipped cream, seasoned with red pepper and add a teaspoon of salt.

Spread the buttered bread with the leaves of lettuce and put on a scoop of the mixture on top.

Add another slice of bread.

These sandwiches may be served in squares tied together with ribbon, or they may be pressed and cut into long narrow pieces. Of course, they must be made only a short time before serving.

The Ton Lobster Sandwiches

For these sandwiches use whole wheat bread.

Instructions

Plunge the lobster into hot water; bring to boiling point, and simmer gently three-quarters of an hour.

Allow to cool.

Remove the lobster meat and dice it fine. Sprinkle with a little salt, red pepper and a tablespoon of tarragon vinegar.

Allow it to stand for a few minutes, and then pour over two or three tablespoons of melted butter. Chill mixture for an hour.

When chilled spread mixture over a slice of buttered bread.

Cover with another slice of bread.

Press the two slices together, and remove the crusts.

Cut into fingers to serve.

West End Lobster Salad Sandwiches

Instructions

Cut the lobster meat fine and put it into a bowl.

Dust it lightly with salt and pepper and sprinkle over two tablespoons of lemon juice.

Make half a cup of mayonnaise by whisking together one egg yolk eight tablespoons of olive oil.

Select the crispest lettuce leaves, wash and set aside to dry.

Mix the mayonnaise with the lobster and spread a thin layer over a slice of buttered bread.

Cover with a lettuce leaf.

Put another thin layer of lobster on top of the lettuce leaf, then a second slice of buttered bread.

Press firmly together. Cut off the crusts.

Cut the sandwiches into halves long ways, or into three fingers to serve.

Lady Brighton's Sandwiches

Instructions

Chop half a pound of cold, cooked mutton very fine.

To the mutton add two tablespoons of cream or olive oil, a tablespoon of capers, half a teaspoon of salt, and a dash of pepper.

Mix thoroughly.

Use thick slices of bread with the crusts removed.

Spread the mutton mixture thickly on the bottom slice of bread.

In each corner put a mint leaf.

Place the other slice of buttered bread on top and press the two together.

Cut from corner to corner making four triangles. Serve.

These sandwiches may also be flavored with tomato ketchup.

Instructions

Cut slices of brown bread into rounds or circles with an ordinary cake cutter.

Finely chop one-half pound of cooked mutton.

Add two tablespoons of olive oil, half a teaspoon of salt, and a dash of paprika.

Peel and slice four or five tomatoes. Push out the seeds.

Put a slice of tomato on top of a round of bread.

Fill the space from which you have taken the seeds with the mutton mixture.

Add a small lettuce leaf, and in the center of that half a teaspoon of mayonnaise dressing.

Put on top another round of buttered bread, and press the two together. Cut into fingers to serve.

Nice for luncheon on a warm day.

Bonnet Cottage Sandwiches

Instructions

Chop two cups of cold boiled mutton.

Add to it two tablespoons of capers, a half teaspoon of salt, six tablespoons of cream or olive oil and a half teaspoon of pepper.

Mash.

Spread mixture between layers of buttered bread.

Trim the crusts and cut into triangles to serve.

Badminton Peanut-Butter Sandwiches

Instructions

Mix one cup of peanut butter with two tablespoons of olive oil and one tablespoon of chopped pimientos.

Spread this on a slice of unbuttered brown bread.

Cover with finely chopped cress or shredded lettuce.

Add a slice of buttered bread.

Press the two slices together.

Trim the crusts and cut into fingers an inch wide to serve.

Royal Partridge Sandwiches

Instructions

Bake four partridge breasts.

Chop the cooked meat rather fine.

Mash two sardines to a paste while gradually adding two tablespoons of soft butter, a dash of red pepper and half a teaspoon of salt.

Spread the bread slices with the sardine paste.

Then sprinkle over the chopped partridge.

Dust this with salt and a little pepper.

Cover with another slice of bread.

Press lightly together.

Trim into shapes to serve.

Hyde Park Picnic Sandwiches

Instructions

Make a round opening in the top of two French rolls.

Scoop out the bread from the inside, leaving the roll in shape with a very small opening on top.

Save the little piece of crust from the top of the opening.

In a blender, mix together four olives, one gherkin, a tablespoon of capers and one large green, sweet pepper.

Finely chop two ounces of ham, and mix it with the same amount of cooked chicken, also chopped fine.

Mix together with the olive mixture, and moisten with a well-made mayonnaise dressing.

Fill the roll with this mixture. Put on the crust top.

Arrange buns neatly on a napkin in a wicker basket; serve at once.

Cambridge Sandwiches

Instructions

Butter an equal quantity of white and whole wheat bread.

Cut cooked corned beef into very thin slices.

Place on a slice of buttered bread.

Spread the corned beef with a teaspoon of creamed horseradish sauce, cover with watercress leaves, or a crisp lettuce leaf.

Add on a slice of whole wheat bread.

Press the two bread slices together.

Trim the crusts and cut into fingers about one inch wide to serve.

Hermitage Horseradish Sauce

Instructions

Stir thick, dry whipped cream into dry horseradish.

If the horseradish is in vinegar, press out the vinegar and then fold in the whipped cream.

Eton Potato Sandwiches

Instructions

Mash four good-sized boiled potatoes.

Add a level teaspoon of salt, four tablespoons of thick cream, and the yolks of four hard-boiled eggs rubbed to a smooth paste, half a teaspoon of pepper and two tablespoons of olive oil.

Mix thoroughly until you have a perfectly smooth paste.

Spread paste between slices of brown bread and butter.

Trim off the crusts, and cut into triangles.

Serve with a garnish of watercress or lettuce.

Somerset Spring Lamb Sandwiches

Instructions

In the blender put two cups of cooked lamb meat and the leaves from six stalks of mint.

Blend until smooth.

Add a half teaspoon of salt, two tablespoons of melted butter or cream, and a half teaspoon of pepper. Blend to a paste.

Spread between toasted English muffins.

Put mint leaves on the top of the lamb mixture before putting the muffins together.

Countess of Pembroke Salad Sandwiches

Instructions

Chop half a pound of cold, cooked chicken.

Mix with six tablespoons of mayonnaise dressing.

Add half a teaspoon of salt and a half teaspoon of pepper.

Spread the mixture between thin slices of bread and butter.

Cut into fancy shapes to serve.

Croyden Fair Sardine Sandwiches

Instructions

Take two sardines, remove skin and bones.

Mash.

Add a teaspoon of anchovy paste, a dash of salt and red pepper and the yolks of six hard-boiled eggs.

Blend well and stir in two tablespoons of olive oil.

Butter thick slices of bread and remove crusts.

Cut bread into crescent-shaped pieces and toast gently.

Butter the toasts and cover with the mixture, serve at once.

Mrs. Astor's Sardine Salad Sandwiches

Instructions

Remove the sardines from the oil.

Take off the tails and heads and remove the bones.

Mash them in a bowl.

Add a tablespoon of vinegar, or the same amount of lemon juice.

Spread on thinly sliced buttered bread.

Layer with lettuce or watercress.

Add another slice of bread.

Cut into triangles to serve.

Instructions

Toast slices of one-half inch thick bread.

Butter the slices of bread and trim off the crusts.

Remove skin and bones from the sardines.

Lay them carefully over the toast.

Chop some olives and capers finely and mix together.

Sprinkle these over the sardines.

Dribble a teaspoon of lemon juice over each sandwich.

Cut into any shape you may desire and they are ready to serve.

Countess Katharina Sandwiches

Instructions

Put half a pound of Schmierkase into a bowl. Mix until smooth.

Gradually add four tablespoons of thick cream, two tablespoons of melted butter, half a teaspoon of salt, and a half teaspoon of pepper.

Butter half inch thick slices of bread. Trim off the crusts.

Spread with the cheese mixture. Add a slice of pumpernickel or rye bread on top.

Then add another layer of cheese. Add another layer of white bread and butter.

Press the slices lightly together. Cut into three or four finger-shaped sandwiches.

Serve garnished with watercress.

*In arranging them for serving, put a layer of sandwiches and a layer of watercress all through the basket or dish.

Schmierkase (Cheese Spread) Recipe

Instructions

In a double boiler put four cups of dry cottage cheese, one teaspoon soda, one tablespoon butter, one tablespoon of salt and one cup of sweetened cream.

Cook until melted.

Remove from heat.

Add 1 teaspoon of caraway seeds for seasoning.

Keep chilled.

Spanish Affair Sandwiches

Instructions

Blend together the hard-boiled yolks of three eggs and twelve boiled shrimps (shelled).

Add three tablespoons of olive oil or butter, a tablespoon of tomato ketchup, a teaspoon of paprika, four tablespoons of chopped parsley, a half teaspoon of salt, and at last stir in four tablespoons of mayonnaise dressing.

Spread this between thin slices of buttered bread.

Trim the crusts and cut into shapes to serve.

Mr Darcy's Salmon Sandwiches

Instructions

Flake smoked salmon, or open a can of salmon, drain it free from oil and break the fish apart in good-sized flakes.

Sprinkle with salt, pepper and lemon juice.

Butter slices of whole wheat or brown bread, cover with a layer of the salmon, then a thick layer of chopped watercress or shredded celery.

Put a tablespoon of mayonnaise in the middle and cover with another slice of buttered bread.

Press together, trim the crusts and cut into triangles.

Duchess Bernhardt Sandwiches

Instructions

Chop two cups of cold roasted beef.

Mix with a dash of cayenne, a half teaspoon of salt, a tablespoon of tomato ketchup, a tablespoon of mango chutney, two shallots, a half clove of garlic and a tablespoon of olive oil.

Spread this on a thin slice of buttered brown bread.

Cover with watercress.

Add another thin slice of buttered white bread.

Press the two slices of bread together.

Cut into crescents or triangles to serve.

Lady Stanley Sandwiches

Instructions

Cut cold beef loaf or roll into very thin slices.

Bake three or four bananas.

Add creamed horseradish sauce.

Butter white or whole wheat bread.

Layer a slice of beef.

Add a thin layer of the mashed baked banana.

Spread a teaspoon of horseradish sauce over the banana.

Add another slice of bread. Press together. Trim the crusts. Cut into triangles and serve.

West End Salted Beef Sandwiches

Instructions

Whip half a cup of cream until it is very stiff. Set aside.

Put four tablespoons of freshly grated horseradish or horseradish pressed free from vinegar into a bowl.

Add the yolk of an egg and a saltspoonful of salt.

Mix and fold in the whipped cream.

Have ready very thin slices of cold boiled salted beef.

Butter thin slices of bread. Put on a layer of salted beef on the slices of bread.

Add a thin layer of the horseradish sauce.

Add another layer of buttered bread. Press together.

Trim the crusts and cut into triangles to serve.

Instructions

Finely chop cold ham.

To each cupful of ham stir in two tablespoons of melted butter, a dash of red pepper and about one-half teaspoon of crushed onion.

Butter very thin slices of bread and remove the crusts.

Spread with the ham mixture.

Roll each sandwich carefully.

Tie with a narrow ribbon store to serve.

Viscount Tea Biscuit Sandwiches

Instructions

Chop two cups of cold roasted mutton.

Add two solid tomatoes from a can of tomatoes, or two fresh tomatoes, peeled, the seeds pressed out and the flesh chopped fine.

Add half a cup of pine nuts, and sufficient olive oil to bind the mixture together.

Spread this between thin, warm biscuits and serve for afternoon tea or supper.

Sweet Society Sandwiches

Under this heading we place all those dainty sandwiches that are made from thin slices of bread and butter and a jam or fruit filling. They are usually served with chocolate or coffee. They are perfect for an afternoon tea or an evening event.

Ascot Cherry Sandwiches

Instructions

Finely chop a quarter pound of candied cherries.

Add a few drops of orange juice, or sherry.

Mix thoroughly.

Spread over thin slices of bread or crackers.

Arrange neatly on a pretty glass dish, and they are ready to serve.

Brighton Afternoon Tea Sandwiches

Instructions

Blend a pound of dates

Add half a cup of peanut butter

Mix until smooth.

Add four tablespoons of sweetened cream and a tablespoon of orange juice.

Spread this mixture between thin slices of white buttered bread.

Press together.

Trim the crusts and cut into fingers or four small triangles to serve.

Instruction

Split a dozen figs and scrape out the soft portion, discarding the skins.

Blend into a paste.

Butter thin slices of bread and remove the crusts.

Spread the fig paste thickly over the bread.

Roll the bread carefully; press for a moment until there is no danger of the roll opening.

Roll each sandwich in a piece of tissue paper; twist the ends as you would bonbon or they may be tied with a thin ribbon to serve.

Duchess Fruit and Nut Sandwiches

These are perhaps the most attractive of all the sweet sandwiches.

Instructions

Blend together a quarter of a pound of almonds, a half-pound of figs, the same quantity of dates, the same of raisins, and a pound of pecan nuts.

Pack the mixture into a baking tray, pressing it down firmly.

Leave overnight to set.

Use a sharp knife cut the mixture into very thin slices.

Place the slices between two rounds of buttered bread.

Serve with chocolate.

*The combination may be varied using candied cherries, citron or any of the candied fruits may be substituted for the dates and figs. Brazilian and pine nuts may be substituted for a portion of the pecans.

Debutant Sponge Cake Sandwiches

Instructions

Bake a sponge cake in a square loaf.

Cut it into slices a quarter of an inch thick.

Cut the slices into rounds with a small biscuit cutter.

With another small cutter take out the center leaving the ring.

Put this ring on top of a solid round making sort of a patty as it were.

Fill the spaces with a mixture of chopped candied fruit that has been soaked in orange juice overnight. Cover the top with meringue made from the white of an egg and sugar

Put them in the oven to brown.

Serve immediately as the fruit will soften the cake if left too long.

Lady Hyacinth's Fresh Fruit Sandwiches

These sandwiches are exceedingly nice to serve for afternoon teas. They must be used soon after they are made. They will, however, if wrapped in a damp napkin, keep for an hour, but as fruit is soft the bread is liable to become moist, which spoils the sandwich.

Instructions

Butter thin slices of bread.

Layer sliced strawberries, dusted with powdered sugar; or raspberries, or large blackberries cut into halves; or peaches, finely chopped; or apple seasoned with a little salt, pepper, olive oil and lemon juice; or sliced bananas with a dash of lemon juice.

Serve as open sandwiches.

Beau Monde Grape Fruit Sandwiches

Instructions

Spread any crisp cracker with a thin layer of grape fruit marmalade.

Put on top another cracker.

Serve at once.

Debrett's Ginger Sandwiches

Instructions

Blend together four or five pieces of ginger into a paste.

Stir this paste into a half cupful of orange marmalade.

Spread between slices of buttered bread.

Press them together.

Trim the crusts and cut into fingers to serve.

*These are nice for afternoon teas. Ginger and carrot marmalade are also very nice.

Nanny's Nut and Apple Sandwiches

Instructions

Put a half cupful of stewed apples into a bowl.

Add the grated rind of quarter of an orange and one cupful of finely chopped mixed nuts.

Spread this on saltines, or any crisp cracker.

Put on top another cracker and serve at once.

These are very nice for children's parties. Of course, one may also use buttered bread, either white or brown.

Minet Raisin Sandwiches

Instructions

Blend half a pound of seeded raisins.

Add a quarter of a pound of almonds that have been blanched, dried and ground.

Add half a cup of quince jelly.

Mix thoroughly.

Spread between thin slices of buttered white bread.

Cut into fingers to serve.

*These sandwiches are very nice in place of cake for afternoon teas or evening companies.

Canapés

A canapé is a half sandwich, as it were. Minced meats of various kinds are served on one slice of bread. In many books they are called "uncovered sandwiches." Cold Canapés are always placed among the appetizers and served before the soup. They are made of such ingredients as caviar, sardines, anchovies, pickled oysters, pickled lobster, devilled shrimps, or a mixture of one or two of these ingredients.

Canapés can be made with slices of bread cut into fancy shapes, toasted or quickly fried in hot oil, or they may be spread with butter and browned in a quick oven. One slice only is used for each canapé. The mixture is spread on top, the top garnished, and the canapés used at once.

Instructions

Cover a round or square of toast with anchovies that have been mashed and seasoned with a little tomato ketchup.

Put a little chopped celery around the edge as a garnish and send at once to the table.

Convent Garden Caviar Canapés

Instructions

Season the caviar with onion and a very little lemon juice.

Spread over a round or square canapé.

Put chopped onion around the edge.

Garnish the top with a hard-boiled egg.

Place on paper mats and send at once to the table.

*These are used as the first course at lunch or dinner.

Croydon Fair Oyster Canapés

Instructions

Cut slices of bread into squares, toast and remove the crusts.

Remove the hard part from a pint of pickled oysters.

Place oysters over bread, close together and in rotation.

Dust thickly with red pepper.

Put over as a thin covering a highly seasoned sauce mayonnaise, and serve.

Marchioness of Abercorn Fish Canapés

Instructions

Pound a quarter of a pound of cooked fish to a paste.

Season with a few drops of onion juice, a saltspoonful of salt, and a dash of black pepper.

Stir in two tablespoons of tartare sauce.

Spread on six or eight rounds of buttered bread browned in the oven.

Garnish the tops with grated cucumber and send to the table.

Instructions

Cut thick slices of whole wheat or Graham bread, trim the crusts and hollow out the centers.

Mash the hard-boiled yolks of three eggs with a tablespoon of anchovy paste or two anchovies, two tablespoons of butter and a dash of lemon juice.

Cut a dill pickle lengthwise into slices an eighth of an inch thick, then cut these slices into long strips a half-inch wide.

Cut large pickled beets into strips of the same width.

Cut a dozen stuffed olives into halves.

Butter the bread. Fill with the paste.

Layer the strips of dill pickle, leaving one inch between each strip. Cross these with strips of pickled beets.

Put half of a stuffed olive into each square. Serve on paper mats.

*Serve as an appetizer before soup.

Royal Ascot Sardine Canapés

Instructions

Remove the skin and blend the sardines to a paste.

Spread a thick layer of this paste over the top of a round of toasted bread.

Cut one gherkin into very thin slices.

Arrange the gherkin overlapping around the edge.

Put a little finely chopped hard-boiled egg in the center, and they are ready to serve.

Royal Foie Gras Canapés

Instructions

For twenty-four sandwiches take one tureen of foie gras.

Remove the fat, and mash the foie gras to a perfectly smooth paste.

Gradually add four tablespoons of soft, not melted, butter.

Add a dash of cayenne and half a teaspoon of salt and about ten drops of onion juice, and blend together.

Cut slices of bread into fancy shapes and toast; crescents are very pretty.

Cover each slice thickly with this paste.

Garnish with hard-boiled white of egg and olives cut into rings.

Arrange neatly on a platter to serve.

A hot canapé is served in the place of fish or as an entrée. If they are dressed with either fish or shell-fish they will take the place of that course. When made from chicken, sweetbreads or game, should be served as an entrée, following the fish.

Ingredients

The white meat from one boiled chicken

6 large fresh mushrooms

2 level tablespoons of butter

2 level tablespoons of flour

1 pint of milk

2 yolks of hard-boiled eggs

1 level teaspoon of salt

1 saltspoonful of pepper

Instructions

Cut twelve slices of bread. Trim the crusts so the slices will be of even size.

Cut out the centers from one-half the slices, leaving a wall of one inch.- Toast the solid slices.

Brush the untoasted edge of the bread with a little white of egg, lay on the rims and put them in the oven to toast on the upper side.

Slice the mushrooms. Dice the chicken.

Put the butter into a saucepan. Add the mushrooms, toss for a minute until the mushrooms are slightly softened.

Add the flour. Mix. Add the milk, salt and pepper. Cook for ten or fifteen minutes until the mushrooms are cooked. Add the meat.

Arrange each canapé on a square of lace paper on an individual heated dish. Put the mixture in the center.

Garnish with mashed egg yolks. Garnish the very top with a little chopped truffle or a little chopped parsley.

*These are the handsomest of all hot Canapés, and while they are usually served following the soup at dinner, they may be used for the main course at a ladies' luncheon, or at a supper.

Waterloo Fish Canapés

Instructions

Pick apart sufficient cold cooked fish to make a half-pint.

In a saucepan, rub together two level tablespoons of butter and two of flour. Add a half-pint of milk. Stir until boiling. Add half a teaspoon of salt, a teaspoon of soy sauce, a dash of red pepper and half a teaspoon of black pepper. When this is hot, add the fish and four or five finely sliced mushrooms. Continue to heat without stirring until the fish is thoroughly heated. While this is heating, trim the crusts from six slices of bread.

Toast the one side carefully. Mash two large cooked potatoes. Place the mashed potatoes in a pastry bag with a star tube. Pipe the mashed potato in a rope-like form, or in small rosettes, around the edge of the bread on the untoasted side.

Brush the bread with a little melted butter and put them in the oven until the potatoes and bread are a golden brown. Fill the centers with the creamed fish mixture. Serve these on square paper mats on individual plates and send at once to the table. *Canned salmon may be used in the place of fresh boiled fish.

Duke Leinster's Game Canapés

Instructions

Dice two cups of game meat.

Put two tablespoons of butter and two of flour in a saucepan.

Add a half pint of stock. Bring to the boil.

Add a half cup of very finely chopped mushrooms, a tablespoon of chopped ham, a tablespoon of chopped parsley, a level teaspoon of salt and a saltspoonful of pepper.

Bring to the boil. Add the game.

Continue to gently heat until the game has absorbed part of the sauce.

Add two tablespoons of sherry or Madeira.

Toast squares bread and garnish with an edging piped mashed potato.- Fill with the game mixture.

Dust with chopped parsley and send to the table.

Aristocracy Lobster Canapés

Ingredients

1 three-pound lobster

2 egg yolks

2 level tablespoons of butter

2 level tablespoons of flour

1 pint of milk

1 tablespoon of chopped parsley

1 level teaspoon of salt

1 saltspoonful of white pepper

1 pint of mashed potatoes

6 slices of bread

Instructions

Toast the bread.

Pipe the mashed potato around the edge of the toasts using a piping bag.

In a saucepan, rub the butter and flour together.

Add the milk.

Slowly bring to the boil.

Add the seasoning and the lobster.

When very hot, stir in the well-beaten yolks of the eggs.

Stir this until it is smoking hot, but be careful not to boil, or it will curdle.

Fill this on top of the toast that has been garnished with potatoes.

Dust with chopped parsley and send to the table.

*Shrimps may be substituted for lobster.

Windsor Lamb Canapés

Ingredients

1 quart of cooked peas

1 pint cooked chopped lamb

1 blade of mace

2 level tablespoons of butter

2 level tablespoons of flour

1 pint of stock

1 teaspoon of Worcestershire Sauce

1 teaspoon of salt

1 tablespoon of chopped onion

2 tablespoons of claret

1 saltspoonful of pepper

Instructions

Put the butter and onion in a saucepan.

Heat gently. Add the lamb.

Bring to the boil.

Add all the seasoning,

Reduce the heat while you make the Canapés.

Mash the peas; the pulp must be quite dry.

Add a seasoning of salt and pepper and one or two tablespoons of melted butter. Put in a pastry bag.

Toast the bread on one side,

Pipe the peas around the edge of the toasts in rope-like form, or roses, on the untoasted side.

Make the pea border sufficiently high to hold the lamb mixture.

Stand in the oven until the bread is carefully toasted.

Arrange them on lace papers on heated plates.

Fill the center with the lamb mixture and send to the table.

Beau Monde Club-House Sandwiches

Beau Monde Club-house sandwiches may be made in a number of different ways, but are served warm as a rule on bread carefully toasted at the last moment.

Instructions

Layer thinly sliced ham or bacon on top of a square of toasted bread.

Add a thin slice of Holland pickles.

Add on top of that a thin slice of cold roasted chicken or turkey.

Add a leaf of lettuce with a teaspoon of mayonnaise dressing.

Garnish with little pieces of water cress.

Cover this with another slice of buttered toast.

Press the two together, and cut from one corner to another making two large triangles, and send at once to the table.

SCENTED SANDWICHES

There is a group of rather special sandwiches made from thin slices of bread and butter flavored or scented with flowers. Among those in common use are clover, rose and the nasturtium.

Clover Sandwiches

Instructions

To make the scented bread, use an unsliced loaf of bread.

Trim the crust off the entire loaf.

Sit the loaf in a large bowl and cover with clover blossoms.

The butter for these sandwiches is also scented in a similar way.

Put the butter in a piece of cheese cloth and place in a bowl covered over with clover blossoms.

Cover the bowl and chill overnight.

The next morning the bread and butter will have the flavor of clover.

Instructions

For rose-scented sandwiches cover the bread and butter with rose leaves overnight.

Put a few rose petals between the slices when making the sandwiches.

Nasturtium Sandwiches

Cover the bread and butter with nasturtium flowers overnight.

In making the sandwiches place at each corner of the slice a flower, so that in cutting from corner to corner you have a little triangular sandwich holding a nasturtium flower uncut.

Violet Sandwiches

Cover the loaf of bread and butter with violet petals.

More Afternoon Tea Sandwich Ideas

For more great ideas and inspirations for Afternoon Teas sandwiches for receptions and High Tea events visit our website www.howtohightea.com

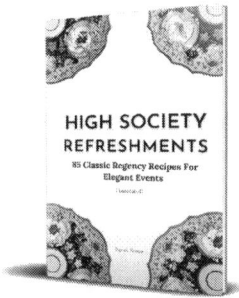

High Society Refreshments

High Society Refreshments is a glimpse into Regency history with recipes including classic savory dishes and sweet desserts that can be served at an elegant society event, as a light meal for an evening dance or for a simple afternoon tea at home. Included are the exact regency cookbook tips on how to serve dishes that are worthy of the most elite society event.and many many more.

Some of the classic Regency England recipes include:

Lady Charlottes's Maple Panachee

Lady Jane's Cranberry Sherbet

Le Dame Chicken Bouillon

Grosvenor Square Lobster Cutlets

Featherington House Chicken Croquettes

Somerset House Scones

Made in the USA
Monee, IL
03 July 2022

99021382R10077